1 Mix medium green for the leaves and stem of the main Violet stencil, and brush it through the stencil using a firm bristled brush with a light stippling movement for the cleanest impression. Neatness matters more with delicate shapes like these.

Stencilling is as easy as painting by numbers. Using fast-drying acrylic artists' colours, and either traditional straight-cut stencil brushes, or firm bristled artists' brushes as shown, follow our step-by-step instructions for perfect results.

THE ART OF FLOWERS

or Easy Steps to Perfect Stencilling

Keep equipment to a minimum to begin with: acrylic colours and bristle brushes available from any art shop, matt white emulsion paint (handy for softening and extending artists' colours), plus masking tape to hold the stencil in place, a plate for mixing colours, and a damp cloth for tidying up any mistakes.

ISOLATE If you only want to use one small stencil element, as here, simply take a little more care when stencilling.

BUILD Adding smaller elements each side of the main Violet stencil creates a completely different shape, which would sit well on a chair back or a bedhead.

2 With a slightly darker shade of green, stipple over some areas of the leaves to give a sense of movement, and emphasise the stems. You may find it useful to use a finer brush for stencilling the stems and tendrils.

3 Use more than one shade of mauve, from pale violet to purple, to bring out the character and form of the Violet flowers. Too pale colours may tend to lose definition.

COMPOSE This pretty informal grouping of stencil elements makes up a unit which can be used as it stands or repeated indefinitely to create a continuous border with a pleasantly irregular and asymmetric movement to it. Violets grow randomly by sending out runners with new plants at their tip, so creating a naturalistic border is easy.

The attractively irregular walls and beams in this cottage bedroom seem to call for a more relaxed use of pattern than a grander room. Instead of being carefully spaced in a regular grid pattern (which gives quite a different effect – and takes much longer) all the stencil elements have been used here in an almost haphazard scattering, as if the window had opened and blown violets all over the room.

EVERYTHING'S COMING UP VIOLETS

Picking up the theme more formally, a parterre of Violets edges a canvas floorcloth, a wreath of tiny buds circles the lampshade, and one perfect plant adorns a prized pillowcase.

HOW DOES YOUR GARDEN GROW?

It's Attention to Detail that Makes the Difference

A posy of ideas to inspire you to use your Violet stencils in all sorts of fresh and attractive ways. Half the fun of stencilling is adding the little decorative details, which only take a minute or so, but give the finished room such a thoughtfully composed look.

Encircling inexpensive card lampshades, and detailing the corners of a painted bedside table; two more ideas for getting the best from your Violet stencil set. When stencilling on furniture, be sure to finish the process by sealing with one or two coats of matt varnish.

This informal composition is achieved by using transparent watercolours with varying intensity, and overlapping stencil elements.

A Violet border makes something very special of a simple painted canvas floorcloth. A variant might be to stencil Violet posies in a lighter colour on a dark painted background.

Paint can do wonders for odd bits of junk furniture; here a Victorian whatnot has been given an exciting Crackle glaze finish, in white over pale blue, and a little Violet stencil has been casually dropped at each corner.

Airy drifts of translucent muslin make a delightful sheer background for a scattering of stencilled Violets. People are often nervous of stencilling on to fabric, but it is just as easy as stencilling any other surface. Use good fabric paints, like Dylon Colourfun or Le Franc & Bougeois, which can be 'fixed' by pressing with a warm iron. With sheer fabrics like muslin, stretch the fabric over clean paper (old wallpaper for instance) so that you have a flat surface to stencil and the surface below is protected from excess paint passing through the sheer fabric.